what would you ask?
NEIL ARMSTRONG

Anita Ganeri
Illustrated by Liz Roberts

Thameside Press

Distributed in the United States by
Smart Apple Media
123 South Broad Street
Mankato, Minnesota 56001

Text copyright © Anita Ganeri 1999

Editors: Veronica Ross & Claire Edwards
Designer: Simeen Karim
Illustrator: Liz Roberts
Consultant: Hester Collicutt

Printed in China

ISBN: 1-929298-03-X
Library of Congress Catalog Card Number 99-73401

10 9 8 7 6 5 4 3 2 1

Contents

What do you do?

"I am an American astronaut and pilot."

On July 20, 1969, the American astronaut Neil Armstrong became the first person to set foot on the Moon. Watched by millions of television viewers all over the world, Armstrong stepped out of the lunar module and took his first steps on the Moon's surface. "That's one small step for a man," he said, "one giant leap for mankind."

In 1957, the Soviets sent the first man-made satellite, *Sputnik 1*, into space. In 1961, the Soviet cosmonaut Yuri Gagarin became the first person in space. This placed the Soviets ahead of their American rivals in the "space race." The U.S.A. was determined to take the lead. In May 1961, President John F. Kennedy announced that America would put a man on the Moon by 1970.

The *Apollo 11* mission to the Moon was one of the most exciting journeys ever made. It was also one of the riskiest. No one knew exactly what the astronauts would find on the Moon, or if they would ever come back again.

Where were you born?

"I was born on my grandparents' farm, near Wapakoneta, Ohio."

Neil Alden Armstrong was born on August 5, 1930, on his grandparents' farm just outside the town of Wapakoneta, Ohio. His parents' names were Stephen and Viola Armstrong. Neil had a younger sister, June, and a younger brother, Dean.

Stephen Armstrong worked as an accountant for the state of Ohio. Because of his job, the family often had to move from house to house.

Neil was interested in flying from a very young age. When he was just two years old, his parents took him to watch the airplanes taking off and landing at Cleveland Municipal Airport. He was so fascinated by the planes that he did not want to leave.

Neil had to wait another four years for his first airplane flight. One Sunday morning, he was taken up by a pilot who was in town to give plane rides to local people.

What were you like at school?

"I always worked hard and wanted to do well."

By the time Neil started school, he could already read. In grade school, he was a very bright student. Neil enjoyed going to school and playing football with his friends. He also became a boy scout. But there was something he enjoyed even more—making model airplanes.

Neil made his first model plane when he was eight years old and was soon hard at work on the next. At the age of ten, Neil got his first part-time job, mowing the grass in the local cemetery. He wanted to earn enough money to pay for new and bigger planes. Later, he worked in a bakery, using his wages to buy a baritone, which he played in the school band.

In high school in Wapakoneta, Neil worked hard, especially in science and math. He was a natural leader, and other students often came to him for help. Neil continued to play in the school band and work at various jobs. Juggling school and work was tiring, but Neil did not mind. After all, the money would pay for flying lessons!

How old were you when you started to fly?

"I was 16 years old when I qualified as a pilot."

On August 5, 1946, Neil celebrated his sixteenth birthday by earning his pilot's license. Flying was like a dream come true, but Neil was also fascinated by how planes worked. After high school, he went to Purdue University to study aeronautic engineering.

A year and a half later, however, the Navy wanted him to train as a fighter pilot in the Korean War. At the age of 20, he was the youngest pilot in his squadron.

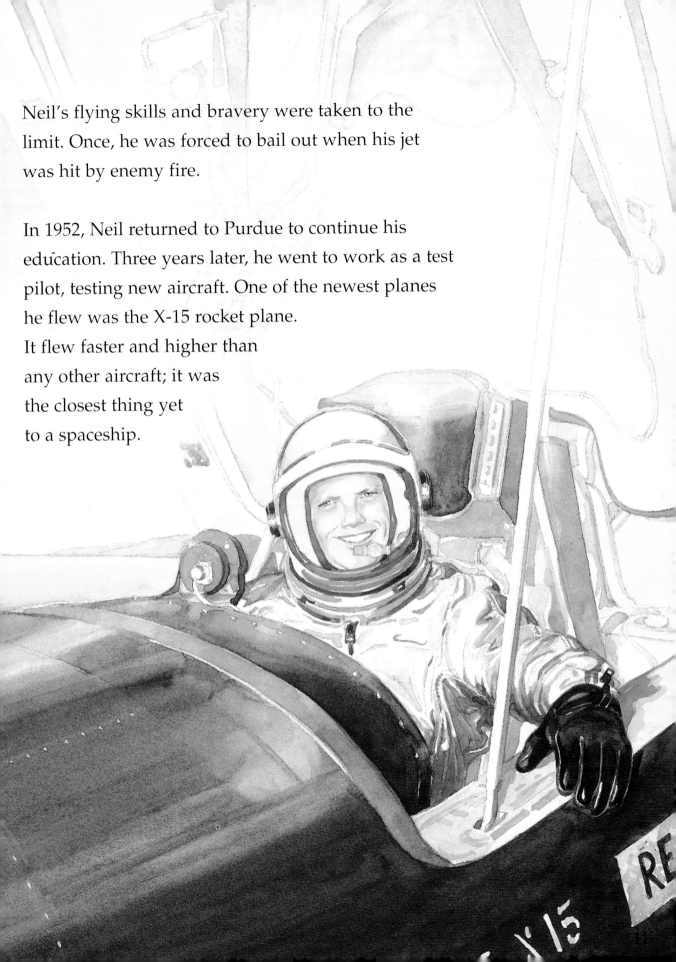

Neil's flying skills and bravery were taken to the limit. Once, he was forced to bail out when his jet was hit by enemy fire.

In 1952, Neil returned to Purdue to continue his education. Three years later, he went to work as a test pilot, testing new aircraft. One of the newest planes he flew was the X-15 rocket plane. It flew faster and higher than any other aircraft; it was the closest thing yet to a spaceship.

How did you become an astronaut?

"I was picked by NASA for the *Gemini 8* mission."

In the 1960s, a series of space flights known as the *Gemini* Project was begun. Neil applied to become an astronaut and was accepted. His first flight in 1966 was aboard *Gemini 8*, which carried out the first successful mission to link up with another rocket in space. At first, things went smoothly. Then one of the thrusters failed and *Gemini 8* started to spin out of control. Neil managed to steady it and avoid disaster, but it had been close.

Neil was praised for his quick thinking and skill. When NASA announced the crews for the *Apollo* flights, he was named the commander of *Apollo 11*, the first mission to land on the Moon. The other crew members were Edwin "Buzz" Aldrin and Michael Collins.

The astronauts began a tough training program. They had to get into top shape—physically and mentally—and learn every detail of the mission. Most importantly, they had to know what to do in an emergency. Neil had no fears about the mission, but added, "What I really want to be, in all honesty, is the first man back from the Moon."

How did you get to the Moon?

"We traveled in a *Saturn V* space rocket."

On July 16, 1969, Armstrong, Aldrin, and Collins
got up early and had steak and eggs for breakfast.
Then they put their space suits on and were driven to
Cape Kennedy, Florida. Standing on the launch pad was
the giant *Saturn V* rocket, which would blast them into
space. The *Apollo 11* spacecraft was perched on top.

At 6:52 a.m., Armstrong entered *Apollo 11*,
followed by Aldrin and Collins. Mission
control started the countdown. "Twelve,
eleven, ten, nine …" *Saturn V*'s
enormous engines began to fire
up. "… six, five, four, three, two,
one, zero, all engines running."
The ground shook, and, with
a deafening roar, *Saturn V*
blasted into the air. It
was 9:32 a.m. "Liftoff!
We have a liftoff …
Liftoff on *Apollo 11*."

Within a few minutes of liftoff, the rocket's first- and second-stage engines had fired and fallen away. At 9:44 a.m., the third-stage engines fired, sending the spacecraft into orbit around the Earth. About two and a half hours later, they fired again, boosting the speed of *Apollo 11* to over 24,000 miles per hour. The astronauts were on their way to the Moon!

When did you step onto the Moon?

"On July 20, 1969, at precisely 10:56 a.m."

After three days of traveling through space, *Apollo 11* went into orbit around the Moon. The next day, Armstrong and Aldrin put their space suits on and crawled into the lunar module, the *Eagle*. At 1:46 p.m., the *Eagle* began its descent to the Moon's surface. All went well, and the *Eagle* made a perfect landing near the Sea of Tranquility. The first words sent back to Earth were "Houston. Tranquility Base here. The *Eagle* has landed."

Armstrong and Aldrin ate a meal, then each put on his helmet, gloves, and life-support system. There is no air or water on the Moon, and temperatures range from freezing to 120°C (248°F). Their backpacks had an oxygen supply, temperature control, and two-way radio. Without these, the men would not survive. Finally, they opened the hatch, and Neil began to climb down the ladder outside.

What did you do on the Moon?

"We collected samples of Moon rock."

Soon, Neil was joined by Buzz Aldrin. Their space suits were bulky, but there was little gravity, so they were able to move around easily. The surface was powdery but firm.

The two men set up a camera and started work. They only had a few hours before their supplies would run out. They collected samples of Moon rock and dust, and they set up a series of experiments. These would help scientists measure the distance between the Earth and the Moon more accurately and build up a better picture of the Moon's surface. Armstrong and Aldrin also put up an American flag. Because there is no wind on the Moon, they had to stiffen it with wire. They even got a telephone call from the President!

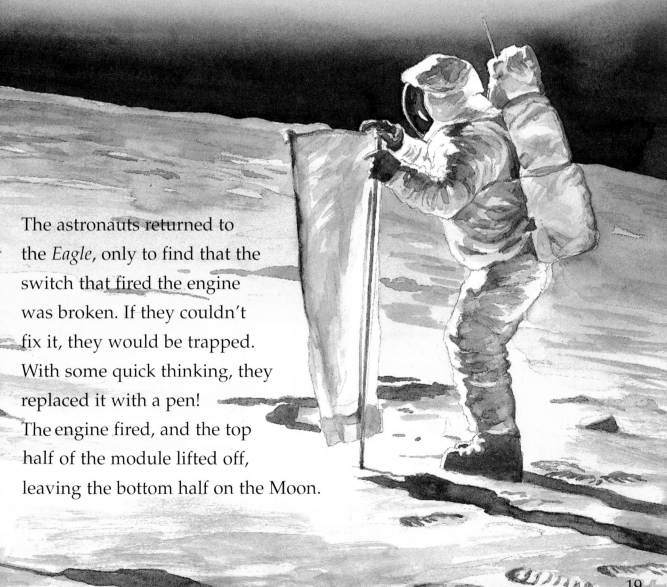

The astronauts returned to the *Eagle*, only to find that the switch that fired the engine was broken. If they couldn't fix it, they would be trapped. With some quick thinking, they replaced it with a pen! The engine fired, and the top half of the module lifted off, leaving the bottom half on the Moon.

How long did you stay in space?

"We were up there for eight days."

Three hours after leaving the Moon, the *Eagle* reached the waiting command module, *Columbia*. Here, the astronauts were reunited with Michael Collins. The *Eagle* was sent into space, to crash on the Moon's surface. Then they began their journey back to Earth. As they approached the Earth, the service module was also jettisoned.

On July 24, eight days after leaving the Earth, *Columbia*'s parachutes opened and it splashed down in the Pacific Ocean. Divers wearing special protective suits opened the hatch, and the astronauts were taken by a helicopter to a rescue ship. The first journey to the Moon had been a success.

Scientists were afraid that the astronauts might have brought back some dangerous, unknown "Moon-germs," which might cause diseases on Earth. So the three men had to spend the next 18 days in quarantine inside a laboratory in Houston. They spent much of this time discussing their flight with people from NASA.

When the doctors were convinced that they didn't have any strange germs, the astronauts were finally allowed out to meet the world and be welcomed back by their families.

What happened when you got back to Earth?

"It was amazing. We were treated like heroes."

The Moon mission had made Armstrong, Aldrin, and Collins famous. Everyone wanted to see them or hear what they had to say about their experiences.

On August 13, the three men and their wives went to three American cities in one day, on a whirlwind tour. They began in New York and then went on to Chicago and Los Angeles. They were also awarded the Presidential Medal of Freedom, the highest award for an American civilian.

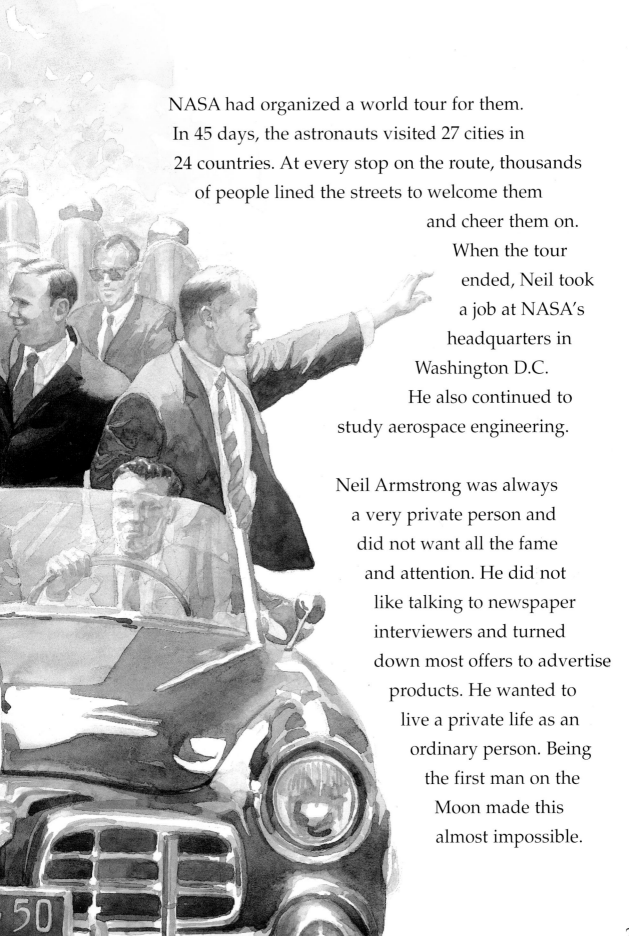

NASA had organized a world tour for them. In 45 days, the astronauts visited 27 cities in 24 countries. At every stop on the route, thousands of people lined the streets to welcome them and cheer them on. When the tour ended, Neil took a job at NASA's headquarters in Washington D.C. He also continued to study aerospace engineering.

Neil Armstrong was always a very private person and did not want all the fame and attention. He did not like talking to newspaper interviewers and turned down most offers to advertise products. He wanted to live a private life as an ordinary person. Being the first man on the Moon made this almost impossible.

Did you ever go into space again?

"No, but I often wished
I was up there."

In 1971, Neil resigned from NASA and taught aerospace
engineering at the University of Cincinnati. He also studied how
space technology could be used on Earth. In 1976, he was the head
of a team developing a pump for use in open-heart surgery. It was
based on a pump used in the *Apollo* space suits.

Neil never went into space again. He bought a farm in Ohio and
lived a quiet life with his family. He rarely appeared in public or
gave interviews. In 1979, he resigned from his teaching job at the
university. Meanwhile, the *Apollo* program continued with six more
Moon missions. The next major step in space exploration came in
the 1970s with the launch of the Soviet and American space stations.

Neil was still interested in space, and he worked on a program to take space exploration into the twenty-first century, though the plan was never completed. On January 28, 1986, the space shuttle *Challenger* exploded seconds after liftoff. Neil was the deputy chief of the committee that was set up to find out what caused the disaster.

In July 1994, people all over America celebrated the twenty-fifth anniversary of the first Moon landing. Neil Armstrong did not take part in any of the official events. He did appear at a local air show. When Neil saw a plane fly overhead, someone heard him say, "I wish I was up there."

Saturn V

The gigantic *Saturn V* rocket was the rocket that carried the *Apollo 11* astronauts into space.

Saturn V was built in three stages, with the *Apollo 11* spacecraft on top. The rocket was 68.7 feet tall and weighed almost 3,200 tons. It was the largest rocket ever built.

After liftoff, the first-stage engines fired for two and a half minutes, lifting the rocket to a height of about 37 miles. Then the first-stage rockets fell into the Atlantic Ocean.

first-stage rocket

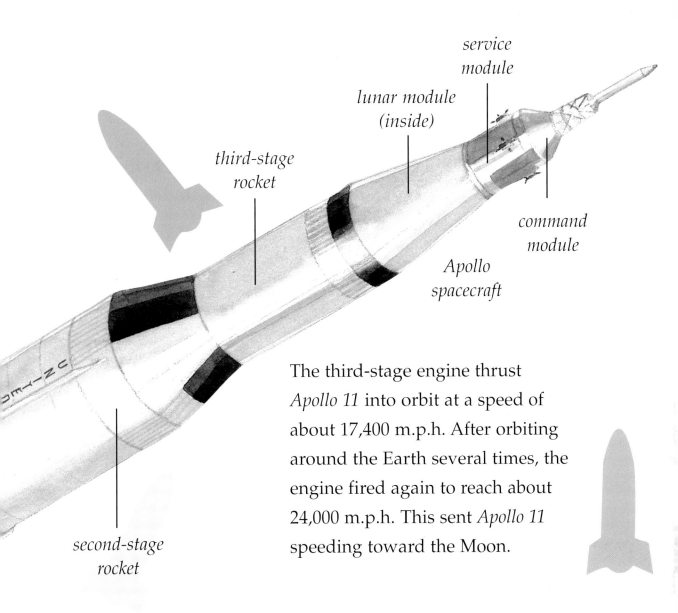

service
module

lunar module
(inside)

third-stage
rocket

command
module

Apollo
spacecraft

second-stage
rocket

The third-stage engine thrust *Apollo 11* into orbit at a speed of about 17,400 m.p.h. After orbiting around the Earth several times, the engine fired again to reach about 24,000 m.p.h. This sent *Apollo 11* speeding toward the Moon.

The second-stage engines burned for about six minutes, taking the rocket to a height of about 115 miles at a speed of about 15,500 m.p.h. Then the second-stage engines fell away.

The only part of the *Apollo 11* to return to Earth was the command module with the three astronauts on board. It splashed into the Pacific Ocean, attached to parachutes.

Some important dates

1930 Neil Armstrong is born on August 5.

1936 Neil takes his first ride in an airplane. He is already fascinated by flying.

1946 On his sixteenth birthday, Neil gets his pilot's license—before he passes his driving test.

1947 Neil graduates from high school. He wins a Navy scholarship and goes to Purdue University to study aeronautic engineering.

1949 The Navy requires Neil to train to fight in the Korean War.

1950–1953 The Korean War is fought in the Far East, between the U.S.A. and 19 other nations. Neil is sent to Korea as a fighter pilot and is awarded three air medals for outstanding service.

1952 Neil returns to the U.S.A. He continues his studies at Purdue.

1955 Neil graduates from Purdue with a Bachelor of Science degree. He starts work as a research pilot.

1956 On January 28, Neil marries Jan Sheardon.

1957 With the launch of the Soviet satellite, *Sputnik 1*, the "space race" between the U.S.S.R. and the U.S.A. begins.

1961 The Soviet cosmonaut, Yuri Gagarin, becomes the first person in space.

1962 Neil is chosen to be an astronaut. He moves with his family to Houston, Texas. He spends his time training and working on space projects.

1966 Neil is made commander of the *Gemini 8* space mission. The spacecraft is the first to link up with another rocket in space. This is called docking.

1969 *Apollo 11* is launched on July 16. On July 20, Neil is the first person on the Moon. He is followed by Buzz Aldrin.

1971 Neil leaves NASA and becomes a professor at Cincinnati University. He buys a farm near Lebanon, Ohio.

1978 Neil receives the Congressional Space Medal of Honor.

1979–1982 Neil leaves Cincinnati University. He serves on the board of various companies.

1984 Neil works for the National Commission on Space (NCOS).

1986 The space shuttle *Challenger* explodes seconds after liftoff, killing all seven astronauts on board. Neil is part of the team finding out what happened.

1994 Celebrations are held all across the U.S. to mark the twenty-fifth anniversary of the Moon landing, but Neil does not take part.

1998 The American astronaut John Glenn goes into space again, on board the shuttle. At the age of 77, he is the oldest person in space. His mission is to test the effect of space on growing old.

Glossary

aeronautic engineering
Building aircraft and improving
aircraft design.

aerospace engineering
Building rockets and spacecraft
and improving their design.

Apollo The name given to the
spacecraft that took people to
the Moon. *Apollo* spacecraft were
blasted into space by huge rockets.
The spacecraft was made up of
three parts, the **command module**,
the **lunar module** and the **service
module**.

astronaut Someone who travels
in space.

bail out To jump out of a flying
aircraft in an emergency, using
a parachute.

baritone A low-sounding musical
horn instrument.

civilian Someone who is not
in the armed forces.

command module
The cone-shaped part of the *Apollo*
spacecraft that the astronauts lived
in and used to return to Earth.

cosmonaut The name for
a Russian astronaut.

docking One spacecraft or rocket
joining up with another in space.

fighter pilot Someone who flies
an airplane that is designed to fire
at other aircraft.

gravity A natural force that pulls
objects towards each other.

jettison To throw away, cast off.

launch pad A platform from
which a spacecraft is blasted into
space by the power of a rocket.

life-support system Equipment that keeps a person alive.

lunar module The part of the *Apollo* spacecraft that landed on the Moon.

Mission A special task.

NASA The National Aeronautics and Space Administration. It is the organization that works on space projects.

orbit The path one object takes around another in space.

quarantine To be kept apart from all other people and animals.

rocket A flying machine that is driven by burning gases to power aircraft and spacecraft.

satellite A man-made satellite is an object that is launched into space from Earth. It orbits around the Earth, Moon, and other planets, and sends information to Earth.

service module The part of the *Apollo* spacecraft that carried the rocket engine, fuel, and oxygen.

space shuttle A spacecraft that returns to Earth after each mission and can be used again.

space station A large spacecraft that stays in orbit around Earth for a long time. Astronauts can live and work there, collecting scientific information, and other spacecraft can visit the station.

test pilot Someone who tests aircraft by flying them.

thruster A small rocket that is used to push a spacecraft to the correct height and in the correct direction.

Index